my nature sticker activity book

In the Vegetable Garden

Olivia Cosneau

Translated by
Yolanda Stern Broad

PRINCETON ARCHITECTURAL PRESS, NEW YORK

It's springtime.
Let's plant our garden!

First, gardeners need the right tools:
a hoe for weeding, a rake for leveling
the soil, a dibble for making holes
and transplanting cuttings, a shovel,
a wheelbarrow, a watering can.

 Complete the tools with stickers.

How to grow beautiful salad greens:

Lettuce seeds need warmth to sprout. Put them in little flower pots in a sunny window. After four weeks, transplant the seedlings into the soil of your vegetable garden.

 Color the lettuce seedlings in the shed window.

Use stickers to transplant them to the vegetable garden.

Underground vegetables: tubers...

Tubers are the enlarged ends of underground stems. Yams and potatoes are edible tubers. When you plant them in the ground, they produce new plants. Potatoes were first grown in South America, from where sailors brought them to Europe more than four hundred years ago.

Color the potato flowers.

Stick some more potatoes on the ends of the roots.

...and root vegetables.

Root vegetables are edible plant roots. Radishes and carrots are root vegetables, for example. Sow radish seeds between rows of carrots to keep weeds from growing. Pull out the smallest carrot seedlings. This will leave more room for the bigger ones to grow.

✏️ *Color the carrots. Get rid of the scrawniest carrot seedlings by coloring over them.*

🍅 *Finish the row of radishes with stickers.*

Artichokes are flower vegetables.

Only the artichoke's flowers are edible. Every plant bears three or four flowers. They're harvested when they are still buds, before they have a chance to bloom. Artichokes belong to the thistle family.

Color the leaves.

Stick the missing artichoke flowers at the ends of the stalks.

Grow strawberries in your garden for a yummy treat.

Strawberries begin as small white flowers in May. Soon the flowers turn to ripe red berries! Not only do they taste delicious but they are also very good for you.

Stick strawberries on top of the flowers.

Fruit or vegetable?

Tomatoes are actually fruits—because they have seeds—even though they are used for savory dishes rather than sweet ones in cooking. Use stakes to prevent young tomato plants from dragging on the ground. Plant marigolds around their bases to help keep the soil moist and weed-free, and to repel insects.

 Color the tomatoes.

Stick on some marigolds.

A pickle is a cucumber
that has been preserved in vinegar.

Cucumbers have seeds, so, like tomatoes, they are really fruits and
not vegetables. Use a trellis when growing cucumbers to give them
space to climb. The plants' tendrils will grab hold of the trellis.
Get rid of aphids (plant lice) by planting nasturtiums near cucumbers.

 Color the flowers.
Draw some tendrils.

Stick on some more
cucumbers.

Pumpkins...

There are more than ten thousand kinds of pumpkins and winter squash! They come in all sizes, shapes, and colors. You can make a Halloween jack-o'-lantern out of them. Or you can eat them! Everything in a pumpkin is edible, even its leaves, flowers, and seeds.

 Color the pumpkins. 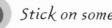 *Stick on some flowers.*

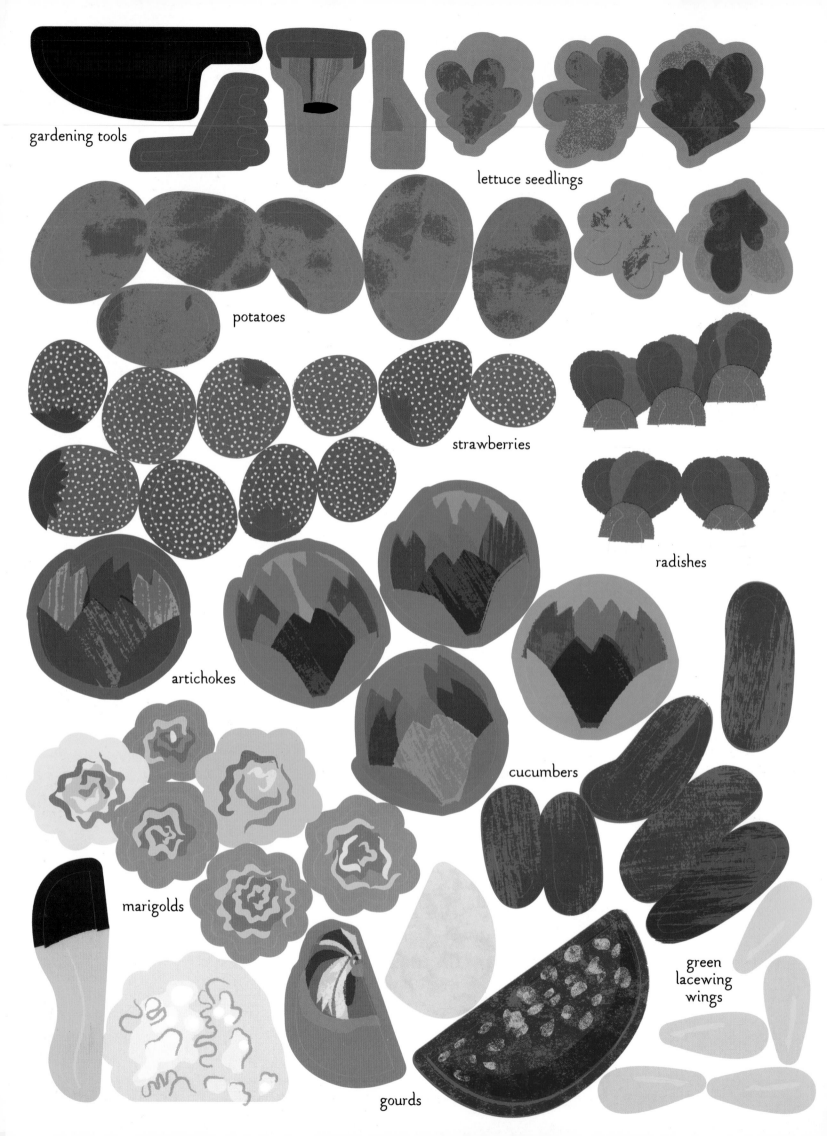

gardening tools

lettuce seedlings

potatoes

strawberries

radishes

artichokes

cucumbers

marigolds

green lacewing wings

gourds

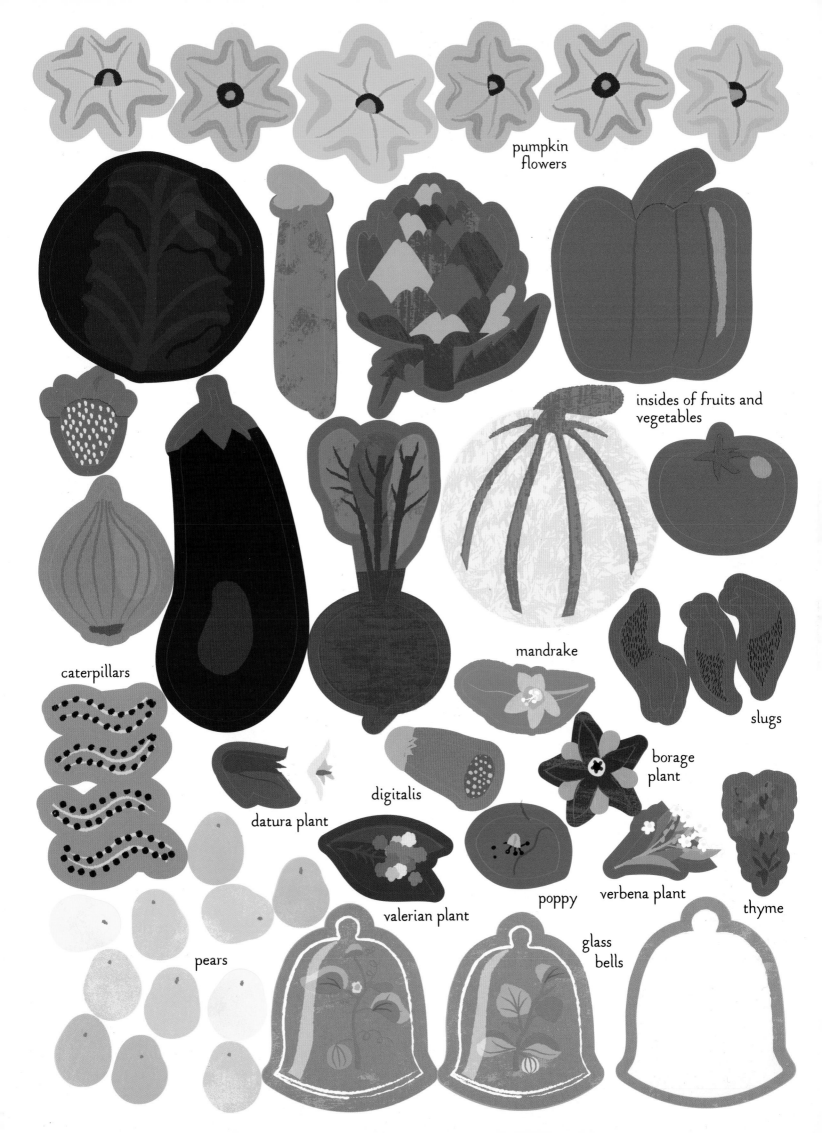

pumpkin
flowers

insides of fruits and
vegetables

mandrake

slugs

caterpillars

borage
plant

digitalis

datura plant

verbena plant

poppy

thyme

valerian plant

pears

glass
bells

...and gourds.

Most gourds are not for eating, but because they come in so many sizes, shapes, and colors, they make great decorations. Grow your own gourds in your garden and harvest them in fall to decorate your home.

 Color the white halves of the gourds.

 Finish the other gourds with stickers.

artichoke

green peas

tomato

pepper

eggplant

What's inside of vegetables and fruits?

Melons and tomatoes have seeds. Cabbages are made out of tightly wrapped layers of leaves. Onion bulbs also have lots of layers. Strawberries wear their seeds on the outside. Their interiors are plump and fleshy. The seeds nestled inside the pea pod are large and sweet.

 Stick every whole vegetable and fruit next to its matching half.

red cabbage

melon

beet

onion

strawberry

Vegetable gardens have enemies...

Birds eat seeds. Slugs love lettuce leaves. Caterpillars have a feast. Aphids suck the sap out of plants, making them wither.

 Color the scarecrow.

Stick caterpillars on the cabbage leaves and some slugs on the lettuce leaves.

...and friends.

When earthworms dig their tunnels, they break up the soil and allow air and water to reach the plants' roots. Hedgehogs eat slugs. Ladybugs and the larvae of green lacewing (also known as stink fly) feed on aphids.

Draw some earthworm tunnels. Draw black dots on the ladybugs. Color the flowers.

Stick wings on the green lacewings.

A king's vegetable garden...

The famous French king Louis XIV, after whom the American state of Louisiana is named, ate summer vegetables even in winter. His gardener, La Quintinie, used manure from the stables to keep the seedling roots warm. When the shoots came up, he put glass bells over them, like little greenhouses, to trap the heat from the sun.

Put glass bells on the melon shoots that don't have one.

...and orchard.

La Quintinie also invented the technique of espaliering by training the branches of fruit trees to grow flat against a wall. That way they stay warm and sheltered from strong winds. Louis XIV loved to eat apples, pears, and figs all year long. Today you don't have to be a king to enjoy fruits and vegetables year-round. But it's best to eat what's in season.

Color the pears and the branches.   *Stick on some more pears.*

The medieval garden.

Back in the Middle Ages, gardens were arranged in square beds, with flowers in one bed (the Mary garden), edible plants in another (the kitchen garden), and medicinal and aromatic plants in a third (the physic garden).

 Color the plants in the garden.

Fix yourself some herbal teas, just like the medieval monks.

Red poppies
for sweet dreams.

Verbena
for digestion.

Thyme
to cure colds.

Borage
for strong fingernails
and hair.

A fourth bed for magic plants.

 Color the magic plants above.

 Stick on the flowers that match the descriptions.

 Datura is a hallucinogenic plant. It made witches feel like they were flying.

 Locking **mandrake** in with your money would double the amount of money.

 Hanging **valerian** in a house kept lightning from striking.

 To ward off the devil, a **digitalis** was planted before dawn.

Test your garden knowledge!

A potato is:
. . . .
- [ ] a fever.
- [ ] a tuber.
- [ ] a humor.

Pumpkin flowers are:
. . . .
- [ ] yellow.
- [ ] red.
- [ ] blue.

La Quintinie was:
. . . .
- [ ] a gardener.
- [ ] a baker.
- [ ] a pastry chef.

People use gourds for:
. . . .
- [ ] decoration.
- [ ] soup.
- [ ] jam.

Artichokes are:
. . . .
- [ ] ferns.
- [ ] thistles.
- [ ] gourds.

Pickles are made from:
. . . .
- [ ] beans.
- [ ] hot peppers.
- [ ] cucumbers.

Carrots are:
- [ ] flower vegetables.
- [ ] fruits.
- [ ] root vegetables.

Earthworm tunnels:
. . . .
- [ ] weaken the soil.
- [ ] are useless.
- [ ] break up the soil.

Aphids are eaten by:
. . . .
- [ ] ladybugs.
- [ ] hedgehogs.
- [ ] slugs.

Turn your activity book upside down for the answers.
. . . .

A potato is a tuber. People use gourds for decoration. Carrots are root vegetables. Pumpkin flowers are yellow. Artichokes are thistles. Earthworm tunnels break up the soil. La Quintinie was a gardener. Pickles are made from cucumbers. Aphids are eaten by ladybugs.